FOSSILS FOR KIDS

Mammuthus sp. fossil

FOSSILS FOR KIDS

A JUNIOR SCIENTIST'S GUIDE TO
Dinosaur Bones, Ancient Animals, and Prehistoric Life on Earth

JUNIOR SCIENTISTS

ASHLEY HALL

callisto publishing
an imprint of Sourcebooks

To my loving parents, Gail and Joe, who sparked my love for museums and never stopped encouraging me to pursue my passion for paleontology.

Author photo courtesy Laura Dempsey.
Illustrations @ Bruce Rankin, 2020, pp. 3, 14, 15, 17, 37, 38, 46, 54; Photography Rafael Dias Trafaniuc/Alamy, p. ii; Phil Degginger/Science Source, pp. viii, 73, 74; Georg Gerster/Science Source, p. vi; Encyclopaedia Britannica/Alamy, p. 2; The Natural History Museum, London/Science Source, pp. 4, 7, 21, 44, 48; Michael Gilday/Alamy, p. 9; Ted Kinsman/Science Source, p. 10; MARK GARLICK/Science Source, pp. 12, 13; Science Stock Photography/Science Source, p. 20; William Mullins/Alamy, p. 23; Millard H. Sharp/Science Source, pp. 24, 25, 28, 31, 41, 45, 77; Francois Gohier/Western Paleontological Labs/Science Source, p. 26; Ivan Vdovin/Alamy, pp. 27, 58; Steve Vidler/Alamy, p. 29; Sabena Jane Blackbird/Alamy, p. 30; Mauricio Anton/Science Source, pp. 34, 35; Kenshu Shimada, p. 42; Roman Uchytel/Science Source, p. 48; RIA Novosti/Science Source, p. 49; John Reader/Science Source, p. 50; Dr. T. E. Thompson/Science Source, pp. 52, 53; Tatiana Dyuvbanova/Alamy, p. 55; Jane Gould/Alamy, p. 55; Larry Pringle/Science Source, p. 59; Hans Gert Broeder/Alamy, p. 60; World History Archive/Alamy, p. 61; Filip Fuxa/Alamy, p. 62; Biophoto Associates/Science Source, pp. 64, 65; Photografiero/iStock, p. 68; Maxine House/Alamy, p. 69; Colin Keates/Dorling Kindersley/Natural History Museum, London, p. 71; blickwinkel/Alamy, p. 72; Louise K. Broman/Science Source, p. 75.
Interior and Cover Designer: Brian Lewis
Art Producer: Tom Hood
Editor: Sabrina Young
Production Manager: Riley Hoffman
Production Editor: Sigi Nacson

Published by Callisto Publishing LLC C/O Sourcebooks LLC
P.O. Box 4410, Naperville, Illinois 60567-4410
(630) 961-3900
callistopublishing.com

This product conforms to all applicable CPSC and CPSIA standards.

Source of Production: Wing King Tong Paper Products Co.Ltd. Shenzhen, Guangdong Province, China
Date of Production: April 2026
Run Number: 5065469

Printed and bound in China
WKT 2

CONTENTS

A paleontologist at the La Brea Tar Pits in Los Angeles, California.

WELCOME, JUNIOR SCIENTIST!

Did you know there are hidden worlds beneath your feet? It's fascinating to think about the weird, wonderful, and amazing animals that evolved thousands, millions, and billions of years before us.

Paleontology is the study of ancient life—it's the science we use to learn about the past. Often when we hear the word "paleontology," we think only of dinosaurs, but there's much more to paleontology than that. In this book, we will "dig" deep into paleontology. From dinosaurs to prehistoric mammals and everything in between, you'll learn where the world's best fossils have been discovered, how paleontologists find and study fossils, and how you can make fossil discoveries of your own.

I'm Ashley Hall, a paleontologist, naturalist, and science communicator. I've loved dinosaurs since I was four years old and always dreamed about working in a natural history museum someday. After I graduated from college, my dreams came true. I've been lucky enough to work in four different natural history museums, as a paleontologist and as a science educator. I've discovered dinosaur eggs in the Montana badlands, uncovered Miocene horse and camel fossils in the California deserts, and studied Ice Age bird fossils at the La Brea Tar Pits in Los Angeles, California. Now I'm excited to share my love and knowledge of paleontology with you.

Do you love fossils, too? Let's dig deeper and learn more about the exciting world of paleontology!

The remains of *Mammuthus columbi* in South Dakota.

Chapter One

WHAT ARE FOSSILS?

Fossils are the remains of ancient life. They help us learn about the history of life on Earth. The Earth is more than 4.5 billion years old and has been home to all forms of life—from microscopic bacteria to the giant blue whale. Bones, shells, insects, plants, footprints, eggs, and even poop (yes, poop!) can become fossils.

Fossils are like puzzle pieces of the Earth's past. The study of fossils is called **paleontology** and paleontologists are the people who piece these fossil puzzles together to learn how plants and animals lived and died, and how life first evolved on our planet.

The **fossil record** is the history of life as told through fossils. But this record is far from complete, and many fossils are waiting to be discovered. That's where YOU come in!

Telling Geologic Time

How do we know that the Earth is more than 4.5 billion years old? Geologists study **geologic time** (the age of the Earth as told through geology) by dividing the Earth into sections of time using **radiometric dating**.

Think of the Earth as a layer cake. Over time, layers of dirt and sediment turn to rock; the bottom layer of rock is the first layer of the "cake." Soon, there are more and more layers until you reach the frosting (the Earth's surface) at the top. The Law of Superposition states that the oldest layer will usually be at the bottom, just like the first layer of a cake.

Geologic time is divided into eons, eras, periods, epochs, and ages. Dinosaurs lived during the Mesozoic Era, which is divided into the Triassic, Jurassic, and Cretaceous Periods.

Geologic time scale, 650 million years ago to the present

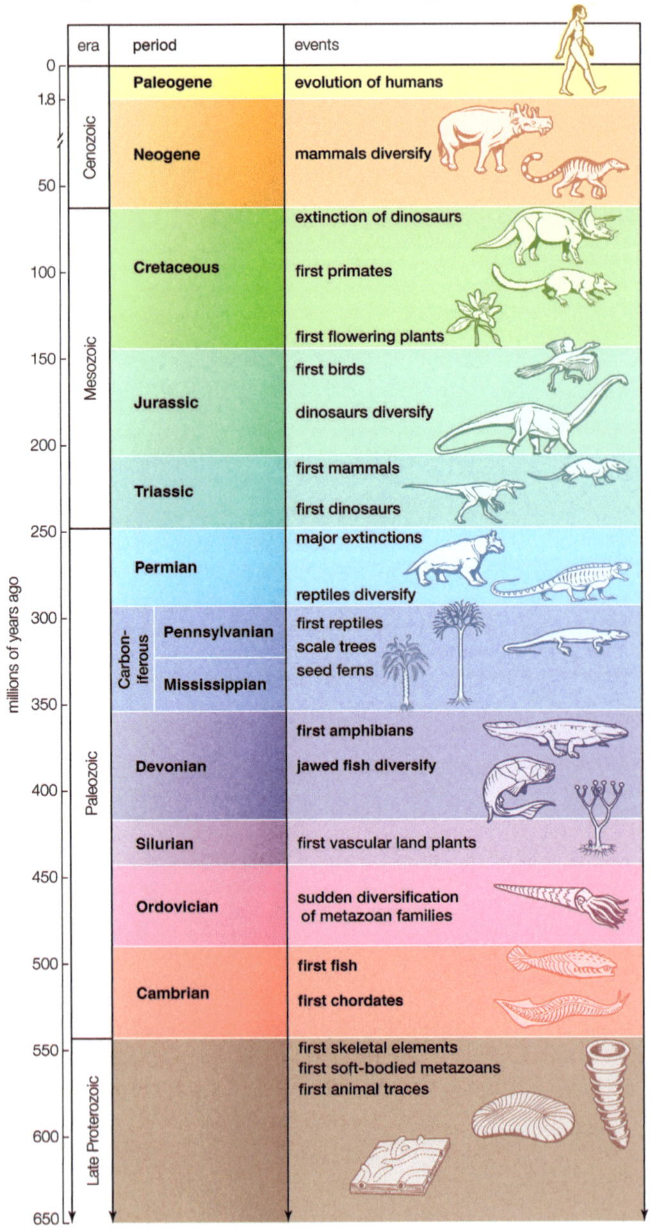

How a Fossil Forms

Fossils are rare! An **organism** needs just the right conditions to become a fossil. Let's explore how fossils are formed.

SILICIFICATION AND PETRIFICATION

Silicification and petrification are the most common types of fossilization. Petrification happens when water carries dissolved, microscopic minerals (like silica, iron, calcite, etc.) into the soft tissues of an organism. Silicification is a form of petrification: The mineral silica, found in volcanic ash, helps preserve fossils.

Living tree

Tree dies and falls over. River floods and buries tree in layer of sand or mud.

Silica-laden groundwater filters down through layers of sediment, replacing organic wood with minerals.

After compression and heat, layers of sediment are eroded, revealing the log that has petrified (become stone).

AMBER

Amber is fossilized tree resin. This thick and sticky resin oozes from tree trunks and branches, trapping anything it touches. As it hardens, it preserves insects, spiders, reptiles, and even dinosaur feathers in perfect condition.

PHOSPHATIZATION

In phosphatization [FOSS-fat-i-ZAY-shun], soft tissues are preserved with the help of an element called phosphorus, which is usually found in living organisms and oceans. Phosphatized fossils preserve lots of details—you might see the cellular structure and soft tissues of the organism. Fossils from the Burgess Shale are great examples of phosphatized fossils.

MUMMIFICATION

Mummification is rare and happens only in special (usually dry) environments. After an animal dies, it dries and hardens, preserving the original skin and tissue. If the mummified fossil is buried by sediment in the right conditions, it may become permineralized (see page 6), or turned to stone. If you see a dinosaur "mummy" in a museum, it might show what the skin, scales, feathers, or spikes looked like when the animal was alive.

THE FOSSIL RECORD

The fossil record is the history of living things preserved as fossils. It's one of the ways we know that the Earth is more than 4 billion years old. Fossils found in the bottom layers of the Earth are always older than fossils found in the top layer. This is called the Law of Superposition and means that the layers of earth and fossils are stacked one on top of another, like a layer cake. If you know what layer (or formation) the fossil was found in, then you can tell how old it is. You can also apply that date to other layers where the same type of fossil is found. Dating the age of these rock layers is called radiometric dating.

The fossil record is far from complete, so every fossil find helps increase our knowledge.

FREEZING

You might have heard that mammoths can be found in ice, still with their skin and fur. It's true! Buried under **perma-frost**, 10,000-year-old mammoths are now thawing out of ice in the Arctic Circle. Mammoths, mastodons, horses, and even wolf pups have been found with their original hair, skin, muscle tissue, internal organs, stomach contents, and even blood!

TAR AND SAND

Tar (or asphalt) is the sticky, thick oil that seeps to the surface through cracks in the ground made by earthquakes. It collects sand and sediment as it rises. This thick mixture of tar and sand can trap living things, preserving them in their original form for thousands of years. The most famous site for asphalt preservation is the La Brea Tar Pits and Museum in Los Angeles, California.

LIMESTONE

Limestone is a **sedimentary** rock that often forms when **exoskeletons** from microscopic marine organisms collect on the ocean floor, or when a mineral called calcium carbonate leaves the water. Limestone contains invertebrate fossils such as clams, snails, ammonites, and corals. Limestone is a popular building material; if you look close enough, you might see tiny fossils in the stones.

PYRITIZATION

Pyritization is another form of **permineralization**. In ocean environments rich in iron and sulfur, invertebrates and plants can become pyritized. Pyrite (known as "fool's gold") is a mineral made of iron and sulfur. Fossils that are formed with pyrite can shine like gold, but pyrite can also cause the fossil to fall apart over time.

Types of Fossils

When we think of fossils, we often imagine a skeleton, but fossils are more than bones. Let's explore the four main types of fossils.

MOLDS

A mold forms when an organism dies and decays, leaving an impression in the surface where it once was. The footprints of dinosaurs are common examples of fossil molds. Molds can either be positive (fills in the fossil form) or negative (leaves an impression of the fossil).

CASTS

As an organism decays, sediment can fill the space, or mold, where the organism once was, taking the exact shape of the original fossil. An invertebrate shell, for example, can be completely filled by sediment, leaving almost no actual shell behind. (A cast can also be a replica of a real fossil, made out of plaster or resin.)

TRUE FORM

True form fossils are organisms preserved in their original form. Dinosaur bones, insects trapped in amber, and an Ice Age mammoth frozen in ice are examples of true form fossils.

TRACE FOSSILS

Have you ever seen a dinosaur footprint? Dinosaur footprints, nests, and even coprolites (that's fossilized poop!) are examples of trace fossils, which are

MICROFOSSILS

Did you know that some fossils are *so* small that they can't be seen by the human eye? These are called microfossils and they are only between 0.001 and 4 millimeters (up to 0.157 inch) in size—smaller than a grain of sand.

What kind of fossils are microfossils? Diatoms [DIE-uh-toms] (single-celled algae), foraminifera [FOR-am-an-IF-er-ah] (single-celled animals), bacteria, pollen, mollusks, and even tiny bones and teeth can be microfossils. Most microfossils are found in marine or ocean environments, but they can also be found in fresh water.

Paleontologists who study microfossils are called micro-paleontologists. They use tools like magnifying glasses, microscopes, and scanning electron microscopes that show the beautiful detail of even the smallest fossils. By studying these microfossils, paleontologists can estimate the age of the Earth's layers and learn about its ancient ecosystems.

called ichnofossils [ICK-no-fossils]. Trace fossils offer clues to an animal's behavior—what it ate, where it lived, how fast it ran, and even what it pooped. These types of fossils help us imagine the lives of animals and plants that lived long ago.

Identifying Fossils

How do you know if you found a fossil?

Where did you find it? Location is important. Fossils are found in sedimentary rocks that are exposed on the surface of the ground. Badlands, beaches, caves, cliffs, deserts, and mountains are great places to look for fossils.

What does it look like? Does it look old, weathered, or worn? Fossils that have been in the ground for a long time can feel and look old.

Still stumped? Ask an expert! If you find a fossil or see a fossil that is too large to be removed, write down the date and the name of the place where you found it. Then take a photo and send it to a nearby museum or university.

Rocks are everywhere, and many people will mistake a funny-looking rock for a fossil. We call these "pseudofossils." How can you tell the difference between a pseudofossil and a real fossil? A real fossil bone may stick to your tongue because of the tiny holes where blood vessels used to be—it's *true* (but don't try this at home). When you find a fossil, sometimes you just know because of a distinct pattern or texture, but identifying fossils takes practice.

In some places, like national or state parks and forests, it is against the law to remove a fossil. Leave your discovery where you found it; instead, write down the location, take a picture of the fossil, and then show both to a naturalist or park ranger. Your discovery might be an important one.

Collecting Fossils

How do paleontologists collect fossils? Very carefully! Paleontologists use rock hammers to chip fossils out of the surrounding rock, brushes to sweep the dust away, dental picks for the delicate work of exposing fossils, and small bags to collect and transport their finds.

When a fragile fossil needs to be removed from the ground, a paleontologist will combine burlap cloth and plaster to make a protective cast, much like a cast for a broken arm or leg. This protects the fossil until it is brought to a museum.

Junior fossil hunters should always bring water, a backpack, a notebook and pencil, sunscreen, and a first-aid kit. Wear a hat, bandana, and some good, sturdy hiking shoes or boots, then go out and explore with your favorite adult!

Where to Find Fossils

You don't have to be a paleontologist to find fossils. With a keen eye, anyone can explore—you just need to know where to look.

You won't find fossils on land covered by grass or trees, because rocks that contain fossils will be covered by plants (so a backyard might not be the right place to look). Most fossils are found preserved in sedimentary rock; this is rock formed from layers of sediment (dirt, soil, etc.) near the Earth's surface. For example, paleontologists look for rocky outcrops. An outcrop is a place where the rock has been exposed due to **erosion** by wind or water. Outcrops are often found near badlands, beaches, caves, deserts, and rivers.

How do you know which fossils might be near you? Look at a geologic map of your state. The **National Geologic Map Database** (Ngmdb.usgs.gov) has maps of the geologic formations in every area. These formations hold clues to the kind of fossils you can find. For example, if you live in Indiana, you won't find any dinosaur fossils, but you might find the fossils of sea life from the Paleozoic Era—that's millions of years older than dinosaurs!

Remember, fossils are rare and finding them takes patience. Don't get frustrated if you don't find anything right away. It takes a keen eye, so keep looking.

Diplodocus

Chapter Two

ALL ABOUT DINOSAURS

Dinosaurs are fascinating, and they make our imaginations run wild. These ancient creatures could be as tall as a four-story building, or as small as a chicken. Some had spectacular spikes or scales, whereas others had frills or even feathers. With their huge teeth and razor-sharp claws, they could eat almost anything—even other dinosaurs. The more we learn about them, the more fascinating they become.

Phylogenetic Tree

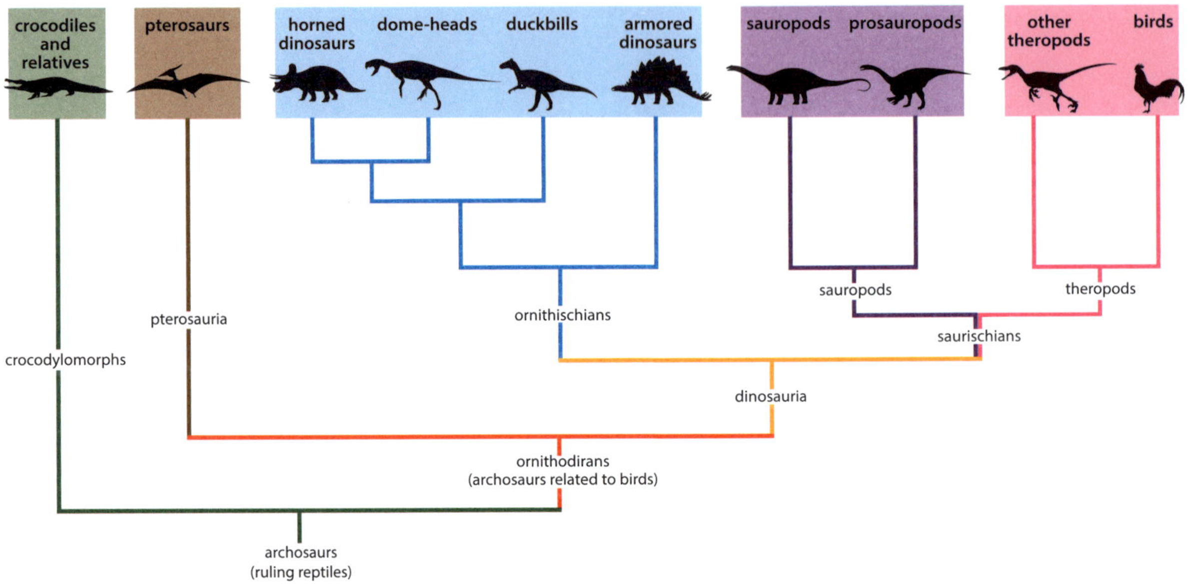

What Is a Dinosaur?

Dinosaurs were a group of reptiles that evolved more than 240 million years ago. All dinosaurs share a common ancestor; this means that they form a group, or **clade**, called Dinosauria. **Ichthyosaurs**, **mosasaurs**, plesiosaurs, pterosaurs, and other groups of reptiles lived alongside the dinosaurs, but were only distant relatives. (They are sometimes mistaken for dinosaurs because they lived during the same time.)

The first dinosaurs were small, carnivorous, and bipedal (two-legged), like *Coelophysis*. Over time, they evolved

to have a wide range of body sizes and diets. Dinosaurs existed for 177 million years until the Cretaceous-Paleogene extinction (66 million years ago). That seems like a long time ago, right? In comparison, humans (*Homo sapiens*) have been around for only 300,000 years.

One group of dinosaurs survived the extinction: birds! Dinosaurs still exist in the form of birds and there are more than 10,000 species of bird living today. The next time you see a bird in your neighborhood, remember that you're looking at a living dinosaur.

Dinosaurs Are Different

What makes dinosaurs different from all other reptiles? Well, one difference is in their hips. When you look at a drawing of a *T. rex* or visit a *Triceratops* skeleton in a museum, you'll notice that

no matter the dinosaur, they all walk with their hind legs directly underneath their body. Other reptiles, like lizards or crocodiles, walk with their legs sprawled out to the side. Paleontologists think that this special hip structure is part of what helped dinosaurs to run, survive, and evolve into the amazing diversity of species we see in the fossil record—and in the skies—today.

All dinosaurs evolved from a common ancestor, but that doesn't mean they are all the same. Dinosaurs fall into two groups—Saurischia [SORE-is-she-uh], the lizard-hipped dinosaurs and Ornithischia [Or-ni-THIS-she-uh], the bird-hipped dinosaurs. Dinosaurs in the group Saurischia have holes in their backbones for air sacs that helped them breathe. Saurischia includes sauropods,

WHAT'S IN A NAME?

Every dinosaur (and every organism) has two names; its genus and species. The genus refers to a larger group of animals that shares similar features. The species name narrows down this group to a specific type of animal. For example, ravens are in the genus *Corvus*, and that includes 45 different species of corvids. *Corvus corax* refers to only one species—the common raven.

Let's look at the *Tyrannosaurus rex*. The word "*Tyrannosaurus*" is the genus and "*rex*" is the species. This system of naming is called a binominal taxonomy, and it was invented in 1758 by the Swedish scientist Carl Linnaeus. To shorten a dinosaur's scientific name, we use the first letter of the genus and then the species name. This is how *Tyrannosaurus rex* becomes *T. rex*.

Now you try it! Can you abbreviate *Allosaurus fragilis*?

meat-eating dinosaurs, and birds. Ornithischian dinosaurs have a backward-pointing hip bone and an extra bone at the front of the lower jaw. Ornithischia includes horned dinosaurs, armored dinosaurs, and hadrosaurs or duck-billed dinosaurs.

What Happened to the Dinosaurs?

Approximately 66 million years ago, an enormous asteroid 10 to 14 kilometers (6 to 9 miles) wide struck the Earth in the Yucatán Peninsula of Mexico. The result of this massive impact was a dust cloud that blocked the light of the sun from the Earth's surface for almost a year. This caused plants and the animals that depended on light and sun, like the dinosaurs, to die. The asteroid's impact also caused tsunamis, floods, wildfires, and freezing temperatures across the planet. Though many of the Earth's species became **extinct**, other species survived and are with us today.

To learn more about the Cretaceous-Paleogene extinction event, read *Asteroid Impact* by author and paleo-artist Douglas Henderson.

Discovering Dinosaurs

How do we know so much about extinct dinosaurs? Fossils! Fossils tell us what dinosaurs looked like, what they ate, and the fact that they ever existed at all.

Dinosaur fossils have been discovered on every continent on the planet—even Antarctica. The most common fossils from dinosaurs are their bones because dinosaurs were

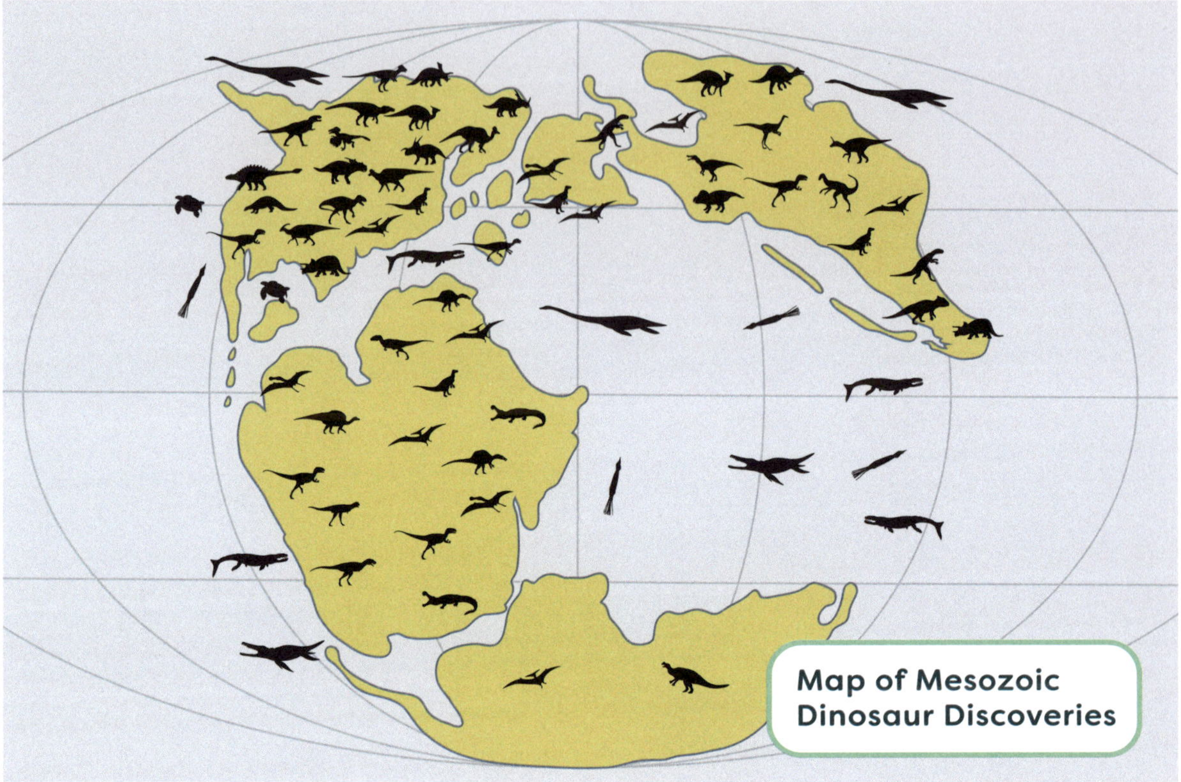

vertebrates, meaning they had a hard skeleton made of minerals. All bones (even yours) are made of the mineral hydroxyapatite. When an animal dies, soft tissues like skin and muscle decay, but the bones remain. Bones can eventually become permineralized; minerals in the groundwater fill the empty spaces inside the bone, creating a fossil. But it's not just bones we find as fossils. Dinosaur eggs, footprints, coprolite (poop), gastroliths (stones in the stomach), and—in rare cases—scales, skin, and pieces of horns and beaks can also be fossils. Invertebrate fossils like shells, snails, and corals are common, but vertebrate fossils are rare, which makes them important to scientific research.

FAMOUS FOSSIL DISCOVERY SITES

Though non-avian (see page 38) dinosaurs are extinct, their fossils are still around. Here are some of the best places to see them:

DINOSAUR NATIONAL MONUMENT (Jensen, Utah): Tour the visitor's center to see hundreds of dinosaur fossils in the famous "Wall of Bones."

DINOSAUR PROVINCIAL PARK (Alberta, Canada): This UNESCO World Heritage Site has yielded the most species of Cretaceous dinosaurs in the world.

MONTANA DINOSAUR TRAIL (Montana): This statewide trail leads to more than 14 dinosaur-themed museums, state parks, and attractions.

ASHFALL FOSSIL BEDS (Royal, Nebraska): Ten to twelve million years ago, a supervolcano erupted, burying ancient rhinoceroses, horses, birds, and camels. You can see paleontologists uncover fossils every summer at this active excavation site.

LA BREA TAR PITS AND MUSEUM (Los Angeles, California): Visit the world's richest Ice Age fossil site, thanks to its sticky, thick asphalt seeps. Paleontologists excavate fossils and work in the lab every day.

Coelophysis

SAY IT! *SEE-lo-FY-sis*

Coelophysis (means "hollow form") was one of the earliest known theropods, or meat-eating, dinosaurs, dating to 205 million years ago. This agile predator was 3 meters (10 feet) long and weighed 15 kilograms (33 pounds). It had a long tail and a skull packed with sharp, serrated teeth. *Coelophysis* was a carnivore; it ran to catch its prey and possibly hunted in groups.

Coelophysis fossils have been found in South Africa, Zimbabwe, and near Ghost Ranch, New Mexico, where a bone bed containing hundreds of *Coelophysis* was discovered in 1947. In 1998, a *Coelophysis* skull was sent aboard the shuttle *Endeavour*—it was the second dinosaur to be sent into space. That skull is now at the Carnegie Museum of Natural History in Pittsburgh, Pennsylvania.

FOSSIL STATS

ORDER: Saurischia

FAMILY: Coelophysidae

GENUS: *Coelophysis*

GEOLOGIC TIME SPAN: Triassic Period, 205 million years ago

FOSSIL TYPE: Body fossil, trace fossil (footprints)

Plateosaurus

SAY IT! *PLAY-tee-uh-SORE-us*

Plateosaurus (means "broad lizard") was one of the earliest members of the sauropod (long-necked) dinosaur family and one of the largest dinosaurs of the Triassic Period. *Plateosaurus* had a small skull, a short neck, and small, muscular arms. Its mouth was full of sharp, leaf-shaped teeth perfect for chewing through tough plants. An adult *Plateosaurus* was 4.8 to 10 meters (16 to 33 feet) long and weighed between 600 and 4,000 kilograms (1,300 and 8,800 pounds). Although its larger sauropod cousins walked on all fours, the bipedal *Plateosaurus* walked upright on its two hind legs.

Plateosaurus fossils have been found at more than 50 sites in Germany, Switzerland, and France, but there are still hundreds (possibly thousands) of *Plateosaurus* skeletons yet to be discovered.

FOSSIL STATS

ORDER: Saurischia

FAMILY: Plateosauridae

GENUS: *Plateosaurus*

GEOLOGIC TIME SPAN: Triassic Period, 214 to 204 million years ago

FOSSIL TYPE: Body fossil, trace fossil (footprints)

DOES BRONTOSAURUS EXIST?

In 1877, famed Yale University paleontologist Othniel Charles Marsh discovered part of a giant sauropod skeleton and he named it *Apatosaurus ajax*. Then, in 1879, he found a similar but larger, more complete skeleton. He named this *Brontosaurus excelsus*.

In 1903, paleontologists realized that the original *Apatosaurus* was a juvenile. This meant that it was probably the same animal as the *Brontosaurus*. Since *Apatosaurus* was discovered first, its name was given priority over *Brontosaurus*.

Despite the change, the name of *Brontosaurus* was more popular (it was used to describe the first mounted skeleton at the American Museum of Natural History in New York City). To this day, the official name is *Apatosaurus*, but everyone still knows (and loves) *Brontosaurus*.

Research update: *Brontosaurus* might exist after all! In 2015, paleontologists studied the original *Brontosaurus* fossils and found that *Brontosaurus* had enough unique features to be its own dinosaur again.

Allosaurus

SAY IT! *AL-oh-SORE-us*

Allosaurus (means "different lizard") had sharp, serrated teeth, strong arms, and a long tail that helped it balance while running. An adult *Allosaurus* was 9.5 to 12 meters (31 to 39 feet) long and weighed 2.3 metric tons (2.5 tons). It may have lived in groups like wolves.

Allosaurus fossils have been found in Utah, Wyoming, New Mexico, Oklahoma, Montana, South Dakota, and Colorado. Utah's Cleveland-Lloyd Dinosaur Quarry is where the most *Allosaurus* fossils have been found—at least 46 individuals. The most famous *Allosaurus* is "Big Al," a 95 percent complete individual. "Big Al" suffered many injuries in life, mostly infections and broken bones, probably as a result of hunting its prey. You can visit "Big Al" at the Museum of the Rockies in Bozeman, Montana.

FOSSIL STATS

ORDER: Saurischia

FAMILY: Allosauridae

GENUS: *Allosaurus*

GEOLOGIC TIME SPAN: Jurassic Period, 155 to 145 million years ago

FOSSIL TYPE: Body fossil, trace fossil (footprints, bite marks)

FOSSIL DISCOVERIES

Brachiosaurus

SAY IT! *BRA-key-oh-SORE-us*

Have you seen the film *Jurassic Park*? If so, you might remember *Brachiosaurus* (means "arm lizard"), the fictional park's gentle giant. This sauropod had a small head, a long neck, and a big body with forearms that were longer than its hind limbs! *Brachiosaurus* weighed between 28.3 and 58 metric tons (31.2 and 64 tons)—roughly the weight of 10 full-grown Asian elephants. Though this dinosaur was heavy, its bones were light and full of air. Sauropod dinosaurs like *Brachiosaurus* had air sacs located throughout their backbone and hips, which made their bodies lighter for their size. These air sacs helped move oxygen through their bodies.

Brachiosaurus fossils have been found in Western Colorado, Wyoming, Oklahoma, and Utah.

FOSSIL STATS

ORDER: Saurischia

FAMILY: Brachiosauridae

GENUS: *Brachiosaurus*

GEOLOGIC TIME SPAN: Late Jurassic Period, 155 to 145 million years ago

FOSSIL TYPE: Body fossil, trace fossil (footprints)

Diplodocus

SAY IT! *Di-PLOD-oh-KUSS*

Diplodocus (means "double beam") was one of the longest dinosaurs, with an extended neck and an extremely long tail that looked almost like a whip. One *Diplodocus carnegii* skeleton measured 27.4 meters (90 feet) long—that's as long as a blue whale—and it weighed between 10 and 16 metric tons (11 and 17.6 tons). *Diplodocus* was an herbivore, which means it ate ferns and tree leaves. It used its thin, pencil-shaped teeth to strip leaves and then swallow them whole. *Diplodocus* replaced each tooth every 35 days—and had as many as five replacement teeth lined up in each tooth socket!

A complete skeleton of *Diplodocus carnegii* is at the Carnegie Museum of Natural History in Pittsburgh, Pennsylvania.

FOSSIL STATS

ORDER: Saurischia

FAMILY: Diplodocidae

GENUS: *Diplodocus*

GEOLOGIC TIME SPAN: Late Jurassic Period, 154 to 152 million years ago

FOSSIL TYPE: Body fossil, trace fossil (footprints)

Stegosaurus

SAY IT! *STEG-oh-SORE-us*

When it comes to flashy dinosaurs, *Stegosaurus* (means "roof lizard") is number one. This iconic dinosaur sported two alternating rows of large, diamond-shaped plates on its back. An adult *Stegosaurus* measured 9 meters (30 feet) long and weighed 5.3 to 7 metric tons (5.8 to 7.7 tons). Though *Stegosaurus* was large, this dinosaur had a small brain—it was the size of a lime!

Stegosaurus fossils have been found in the western United States and in Portugal. Paleontologists have been studying *Stegosaurus* since 1876, but they still don't know what their plates were for. Maybe you can be the one to help solve this mystery.

FOSSIL STATS

ORDER: Ornithischia

FAMILY: Stegosauridae

GENUS: *Stegosaurus*

GEOLOGIC TIME SPAN: Jurassic Period, 155 to 145 million years ago

FOSSIL TYPE: Body fossil, trace fossil

Archaeopteryx

SAY IT! *Ar-key-OP-tuh-riks*

Archaeopteryx (means "ancient wing") is one of the most important fossils ever found. This animal shared features with modern birds and dinosaurs. It had feathers, a **furcula**, hollow thin-walled bones, and air sacs, like a bird. But like dinosaurs, it also had teeth (instead of a beak), a long, bony tail, and three fingers with claws on each hand. Paleontologists know that *Archaeopteryx* could fly, but not as far or as fast as birds today.

Archaeopteryx lived in a series of islands in the middle of a warm, tropical sea—what we now call Germany. (Germany was much closer to the equator back then.) Twelve *Archaeopteryx* fossils have been found, all in limestone deposits near Solnhofen, Germany. The most famous specimen is "the Berlin specimen," *Archaeopteryx lithographica*.

FOSSIL DISCOVERIES

FOSSIL STATS

ORDER: Saurischia	**GEOLOGIC TIME SPAN:** Jurassic Period, 152 to 151 million years ago
FAMILY: Archaeopterygidae	**FOSSIL TYPE:** Body fossil
GENUS: *Archaeopteryx*	

Edmontosaurus

SAY IT! *ED-mon-TOE-sore-us*

Edmontosaurus (means "lizard of Edmonton") was a large hadrosaur—a duck-billed dinosaur. The largest adults were 12 meters (39 feet) long and weighed 4 metric tons (4.4 tons)—almost as large as *T. rex*. (*Edmontosaurus* was a favorite food of *T. rex*.)

Edmontosaurus roamed in great herds across North America; bones and footprints have been found in Montana, North Dakota, South Dakota, Wyoming, Colorado, and Alberta and Saskatchewan, Canada. The first fossils were found in Edmonton, Canada, and so *Edmontosaurus* was named after that city. One of the world's best dinosaur "mummies" is an *Edmontosaurus* found in Wyoming and now at the American Museum of Natural History in New York City—you can even see its petrified skin.

FOSSIL STATS

ORDER: Ornithischia

FAMILY: Hadrosauridae

GENUS: *Edmontosaurus*

GEOLOGIC TIME SPAN: Late Cretaceous Period, 71 to 66 million years ago

FOSSIL TYPE: Body fossil, trace fossil (footprints)

Psittacosaurus

SAY IT! *SIT-tack-oh-SORE-us*

Psittacosaurus (means "parrot lizard") was a small bipedal relative of *Triceratops*. The largest *Psittacosaurus* was only 2 meters (7 feet) long and weighed 20 kilograms (44 pounds), the size of a big dog. It had a short skull with a large parrot-like beak full of small, leaf-shaped teeth that it used to reach tough plants and hard seeds. Scales covered much of its body, but its tail was coated in bristles (quills). *Psittacosaurus*'s skin was counter-shaded. It had dark skin on its face, back, and shoulders, but a lighter skin color on its belly. This counter-shaded coloring helped it hide, or camouflage, in its forest habitat.

Psittacosaurus fossils have been found in China, Mongolia, and Russia.

FOSSIL STATS

ORDER: Ornithischia

FAMILY: Psittacosauridae

GENUS: *Psittacosaurus*

GEOLOGIC TIME SPAN: Early Cretaceous Period, 126 to 101 million years ago

FOSSIL TYPE: Body fossil, trace fossil (gastroliths)

FOSSIL DISCOVERIES

Velociraptor

SAY IT! *Vel-AH-si-RAP-tor*

If the dinosaur *Velociraptor* (means "swift thief") sounds familiar, it might be because they were featured in the film *Jurassic Park*. Those *Velociraptors* were much larger and scarier than an actual *Velociraptor*, which was only the size of a turkey. *Velociraptor* was about 2 meters (7 feet) long—that's including the tail—50 centimeters (2 feet) high at the hip, and weighed 15 kilograms (33 pounds). The discovery of a *Velociraptor* with quill knobs—attachments for the wing feathers on the arms of birds—confirmed that *Velociraptor* had feathers.

Velociraptor was a swift predator; it used its strong arms to catch its prey while pinning it down with large, powerful toe-claws. The most famous specimen was found entangled in battle with *Protoceratops*. The two died together when a sand dune collapsed, preserving them for all time.

FOSSIL STATS

ORDER: Saurischia

FAMILY: Dromaeosauridae

GENUS: *Velociraptor*

GEOLOGIC TIME SPAN: Late Cretaceous Period, 76 to 72 million years ago

FOSSIL TYPE: Body fossil

Triceratops

SAY IT! *Tri-SARAH-tops*

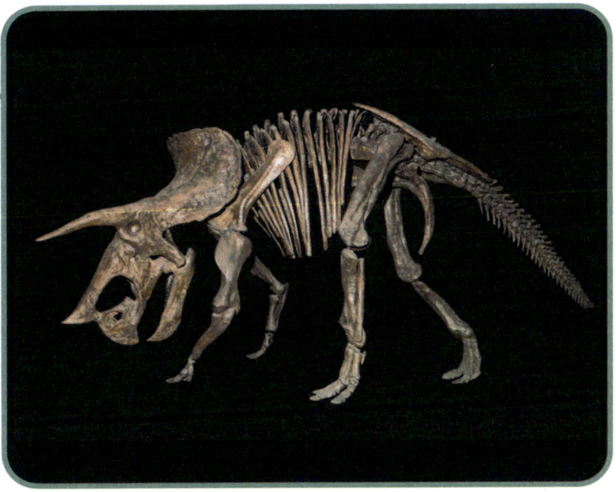

Triceratops (means "three-horned face") is easy to recognize. Just look for three horns, a beak, and a large bony frill around its neck. Adults were 9 meters (30 feet) long and weighed up to 5.5 metric tons (6 tons). *Triceratops* used its horns and intimidating frill to defend itself against *T. rex* and other predators. *T. rex* bite marks have been found on the skulls and pelvis of *Triceratops* fossils—evidence that *Triceratops* didn't always win.

Triceratops fossils are common in Montana, South Dakota, Colorado, Wyoming, and Alberta, Canada. The Museum of the Rockies in Bozeman, Montana, has the best and largest collection of *Triceratops* fossils in the world, from babies to adults.

FOSSIL STATS

ORDER: Ornithischia

FAMILY: Ceratopsidae

GENUS: *Triceratops*

GEOLOGIC TIME SPAN: Late Cretaceous Period, 68 to 66 million years ago

FOSSIL TYPE: Body fossil, trace fossil (footprints)

Tyrannosaurus rex

SAY IT! *Tie-RAN-no-SAWR-us REX*

Tyrannosaurus rex (means "tyrant lizard king"), or *T. rex,* is the most famous dinosaur of all! Although *T. rex* wasn't the largest carnivore, its bite had a force of 6.5 metric tons (7.2 tons)—that's the same force as dropping two pickup trucks at the same time! Paleontologists once thought *T. rex* was a scavenger, but then we discovered that they also hunted live prey. *T. rex* was one of the last dinosaur species alive before the Cretaceous-Paleogene extinction event.

T. rex fossils have been found in Montana, North Dakota, South Dakota, New Mexico, Texas, Utah, Wyoming, and Alberta and Saskatchewan, Canada. The most complete *T. rex* skeleton is called "Sue," discovered in South Dakota. It's on display at the Field Museum of Natural History in Chicago, Illinois.

FOSSIL STATS

ORDER: Saurischia

FAMILY: Tyrannosauridae

GENUS: *Tyrannosaurus*

GEOLOGIC TIME SPAN: Late Cretaceous Period, 68 to 66 million years ago

FOSSIL TYPE: Body fossil and trace fossil (footprints)

TOP FIVE PLACES TO SEE A DINOSAUR

Want to see some of the best dinosaur skeletons ever found? Visit the following museums to see some of your favorite dinosaurs, extinct animals, and more.

1. The **FIELD MUSEUM OF NATURAL HISTORY**, in Chicago, Illinois, is home to "Sue," the most complete *T. rex* in the world!
2. The **SMITHSONIAN NATIONAL MUSEUM OF NATURAL HISTORY**, in Washington, D.C., opened a "Deep Time" exhibition gallery in 2019—perfect for a summer trip.
3. The **AMERICAN MUSEUM OF NATURAL HISTORY**, in New York, New York, has two classic galleries: the Hall of Saurischian Dinosaurs and the Hall of Ornithischian Dinosaurs.
4. The **ACADEMY OF NATURAL SCIENCES OF DREXEL UNIVERSITY**, in Philadelphia, Pennsylvania, is where vertebrate paleontology began. It's also where the Bone Wars, an intense competition between two fossil hunters, took place.
5. The **NATURAL HISTORY MUSEUM**, in London, England, is home to "Sophie," the most complete *Stegosaurus* in the world!

Woolly mammoths

Chapter Three

ALL ABOUT VERTEBRATES

Let's explore the exciting world of animals with backbones—the vertebrates. How do you know whether you are a vertebrate animal? Reach behind yourself and feel your back. Can you feel your spine? Those bumpy bones mean that you are a vertebrate. There are five classes of animals with vertebrae: fish, reptiles, amphibians, birds, and mammals. (These groups include humans and dinosaurs.)

Here's a fun fact: *You* came from a mammal that evolved from a reptile that evolved from an amphibian that evolved from a fish. How the heck did *that* happen?

Where Vertebrates Come From

We can track the evolution of vertebrates by looking at the fossil record. The very beginnings of life on Earth can be traced back to the Precambrian Period (4.6 billion to 541 million years ago). In the Precambrian Period, life was very simple and consisted of mostly single-celled organisms like blue-green algae.

The following Cambrian Period (541 million years ago) saw the Cambrian explosion, a 13-to-25-million-year event when life evolved into an amazing variety of complex cells and body shapes. All vertebrate animals today can trace their ancestry back to the Cambrian Period, including you.

In 1999, a new fossil site from the Cambrian explosion was discovered, and it contained many early vertebrate animals. The Chengjiang biota [CHENG-jang bye-OH-tah] fossil site yielded important new discoveries, including *Haikouichthys* [HI-coo-ICK-theez], an animal 2.5 centimeters (1 inch) long with a slender body, a dorsal fin, gills, a head, and, most important, a **notochord**—the early beginning of a spine. This could be one of our earliest vertebrate ancestors.

Fish

Did you know that more than half of all vertebrates are fish? Fish were the first animals with a true backbone like humans. This bone was mineralized with hard calcium hydroxylapatite [high-DRAWX-cell-APP-ah-tyte] and it gave early vertebrate bodies structural support, as well as places to store nutrients and for muscles to attach. Yet these animals did not have jaws. Jawless fish, or **agnathans**, had a simple circular opening for a mouth similar to modern-day lampreys. Eventually fish evolved movable jaws from their gill arches, and teeth were not far behind.

By the Silurian Period (443 million years ago), fish started to look like the animals we see today. The earliest sharks and armored fish, or **placoderms**, are from this time. These fish had skulls made of thick bony plates.

Then came the Devonian Period (419 million years ago), known as the Age of Fishes. This is when fish diversified, and the oceans filled with many bizarre and wonderful fish like the brushy-finned *Stethacanthus* [STETH-a-can-thus] and the whorl-toothed *Helicoprion* [HELL-uh-cope-ree-on]. *Dunkleosteus terrelli* [DUN-kull-AH-stee-us ter-RELL-eye] is one of the most well-known placoderms from this time.

By the end of the Devonian Period (380 million years ago), fish were starting to explore a new habitat—land!

Reptiles and Amphibians

Many lobe-finned fish, like *Tiktaalik roseae* [Tik-TAH-lick ROW-zee-ay], had fins with such sturdy bones that they could use them to pull themselves onto land! The lobe-finned fish of the Devonian Period were on their way to becoming the first **tetrapods**—the four-legged land-dwelling animals that would eventually include amphibians, reptiles, birds, mammals, and you.

During the Carboniferous Period (358 million years ago), fish and tetrapods filled Earth's fresh waters, but some evolved adaptations to leave the water behind. They grew hard scales instead of soft skin, laid hard-shelled eggs, and had strong limbs for walking and running. By the Permian Period (300 million years ago), amphibians and reptiles had taken over the land. One group of these new scaly vertebrates—the synapsids—would give rise to mammals.

Birds

Birds are **avian** dinosaurs that evolved in the Jurassic Period (more than 150 million years ago). They flew over the heads of dinosaurs in the Mesozoic Era, survived the Cretaceous-Paleogene extinction, and are still alive today. (In fact, one of the most famous fossil birds is *Archaeopteryx* [AR-kee-OP-tery-icks].)

Look around—there are more than 10,000 species of these avian dinosaurs in the skies, in the trees, and some are even kept as pets. Birds are one of the most successful and adaptable groups of animals on the planet.

Mammals

The Permian-Triassic extinction (252 million years ago) wiped out many of the Permian reptile groups. However, this set the stage for a new group of reptiles—dinosaurs. Beginning in the Triassic Period (252 million years ago), dinosaurs dominated the land, whereas other reptiles that could swim or fly took to the sea and the air.

The Jurassic Period (201 to 145 million years ago) also saw small, furry mammals like *Docofossor* [DOC-oh-faw-sir] and *Liaoconodon* [LEE-ow-CON-oh-DON] thrive. These warm-blooded mammals (no bigger than a raccoon) were different from reptiles: Many of them gave birth to live young instead of laying eggs, and they nursed them with milk (like humans and other mammals nurse their babies today). These adaptations have helped mammals survive and thrive to this day.

The end of the Mesozoic Era is marked by the Cretaceous-Paleogene extinction (66 million years ago), when most dinosaurs became extinct. The mammals that survived adapted to the harsh conditions as a result of an asteroid impact—freezing temperatures and a lack of food. These mammals had fur that kept them warm and some raised their babies underground in cozy burrows. They had to survive on very little food and scavenged when possible.

But survive they did. They have since evolved into the amazingly diverse groups of mammals we see today.

FIND OUT MORE!

To learn more about the evolution of vertebrates, check out these free resources:

- The **HOWARD HUGHES MEDICAL INSTITUTE** has free DVDs, a classroom curriculum, and activities about evolution, including paleontologist Neil Shubin's film, *Your Inner Fish* (hhmi.org/education).
- The University of California at Berkeley's **UNDERSTANDING EVOLUTION** website is your one-stop source for evolution education (evolution.berkeley.edu/evolibrary/home.php).
- Learn about evolution—and your favorite extinct animals—by watching the fascinating and educational **PBS *EONS*** video series (pbs.org/show/eons).
- Go behind the scenes of Chicago's amazing Field Museum of Natural History with science educator Emily Graslie in **THE BRAIN SCOOP** YouTube series (youtube.com/user/thebrainscoop).
- The **NATIONAL GEOGRAPHIC KIDS** website uses games, videos, and more to explore all five classes of vertebrates (kids.nationalgeographic.com).

Diplocaulus

SAY IT! *DIP-low-CALL-us*

Diplocaulus (means "double caul") was an amphibian with a boomerang-shaped head. It lived in freshwater streams and rivers around 306 to 255 million years ago. *Diplocaulus* was almost 1 meter (3 feet) long and weighed 4.5 kilograms (10 pounds), about the size of a Chinese giant salamander. It lived in water to keep its skin moist; its boomerang head shape may have helped water flow over its head as it rose from the bottom of streambeds to the water's surface, then went back down again.

Dimetrodon, a sail-back synapsid, appears to have considered this amphibian a yummy snack. Many *Diplocaulus* fossils have been found with partial bites taken out of their heads. Some of the best fossils of *Diplocaulus* can be seen at the Whiteside Museum of Natural History in Seymour, Texas.

FOSSIL DISCOVERIES

FOSSIL STATS

ORDER: Nectridea

FAMILY: Diplocauidae

GENUS: *Diplocaulus*

GEOLOGIC TIME SPAN: Carboniferous Period to late Permian Period, 306 to 255 million years ago

FOSSIL TYPE: Body fossil

Cretalamna

SAY IT! *KRET-ah-LAMB-nuh*

Did you know that sharks lived during the time of the dinosaurs? In fact, sharks are older than dinosaurs as they evolved more than 400 million years ago. *Cretalamna* (means "chalk shark") is a genus—a group of sharks—that may be the ancestor of today's mako and great white sharks, as well as the extinct shark known as "megalodon." *Cretalamna* had sharp teeth with three cusps (or points) that allowed it to eat sea turtles, other sharks, and marine reptiles.

Their teeth have been found stuck in fossil plesiosaur bones, which means these ancient sharks ate and scavenged plesiosaurs. Paleontologists study *Cretalamna* teeth in order to tell different species apart. *Cretalamna* fossils have been found around the world.

FOSSIL STATS

ORDER: Lamniformes

FAMILY: Otodontidae

GENUS: *Cretalamna*

GEOLOGIC TIME SPAN: Early Cretaceous Period to Eocene Period, 103 to 48 million years ago

FOSSIL TYPE: Body fossil

Dunkleosteus

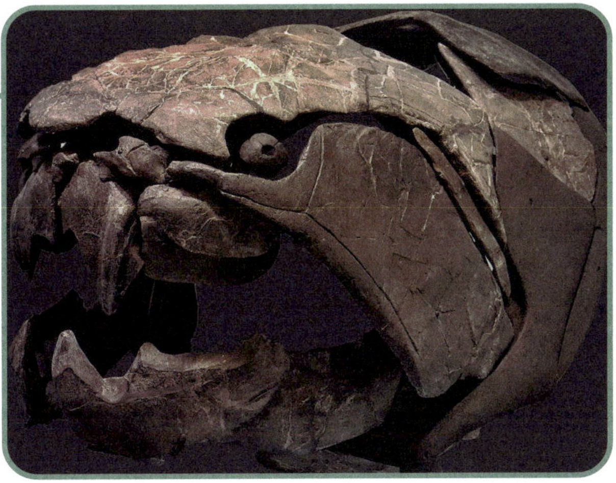

SAY IT! *DUNK-ul-AH-stee-us*

Dunkleosteus terrelli (means "Dunkle's bones") is one of the most impressive predators of all time. Nicknamed "the Cleveland cleaver," *Dunkleosteus* was 6 meters (20 feet) long and weighed 907 kilograms (1 ton). An active predator, *Dunkleosteus* ate sharks like *Cladoselache* [KLAD-oh-sell-ACK-ee] and possibly even other *Dunkleosteus*. (Bite marks from *Dunkleosteus* have been found on the skulls of other *Dunkleosteus*!)

The only fossils we have from *Dunkleosteus* are their skulls. Their bodies were made of cartilage (soft tissue), which decomposed or was eaten by scavengers after death. You can see the best *Dunkleosteus terrelli* fossils in the world at the Cleveland Museum of Natural History in Cleveland, Ohio.

FOSSIL STATS

ORDER: Arthrodira

FAMILY: Dunkleosteidae

GENUS: *Dunkleosteus*

GEOLOGIC TIME SPAN: Devonian Period, 375 to 358 million years ago

FOSSIL TYPE: Body fossil

Hylonomus

SAY IT! *HIGH-low-nome-us*

Back in the Carboniferous Period (315 million years ago), early reptiles began to adapt and move from living in water to living on land. *Hylonomus* (means "forest dweller") is the world's oldest fossil reptile. At only 20 to 25 centimeters (8 to 10 inches) long, *Hylonomus*, with its sharp teeth, four legs, scaly skin, and tail, resembles today's lizards. *Hylonomus* fossils are often found inside the petrified stumps of lycopod trees. Paleontologists aren't sure why they became trapped in these stumps, but they may have been seeking shelter or making nests and were unable to escape.

Fossil footprints made by *Hylonomus* have been discovered in New Brunswick, Canada. The Joggins Fossil Cliffs in Nova Scotia has petrified tree stumps containing *Hylonomus* fossils.

FOSSIL STATS

ORDER: Eureptilia

FAMILY: Romeriida

GENUS: *Hylonomus*

GEOLOGIC TIME SPAN: Carboniferous Period, 315 million years ago

FOSSIL TYPE: Body fossil, trace fossil (footprints)

Pterodactylus

SAY IT! *TARE-oh-DACK-till-us*

Pterodactylus (means "winged finger") was a small pterosaur with a wingspan 1 meter (3 feet) long—the same wingspan as a crow. Pterosaurs were not dinosaurs but were a group of flying reptiles that lived during the Mesozoic Era. Pterosaur wings were made of thin skin that was supported by an elongated fourth finger (like your "ring" finger). *Pterodactylus* were omnivores and ate small animals, insects, and plants.

Pterodactylus antiquus was the first pterosaur discovered; it was described by Italian scientist Cosimo Alessandro Collini in Bavaria in 1784. More than 30 *Pterodactylus* fossils have been found in the Solnhofen Limestone in Germany—the same limestone where we discovered the famous fossil, *Archaeopteryx*.

FOSSIL STATS

ORDER: Pterosauria

FAMILY: Pterodactylidae

GENUS: *Pterodactylus*

GEOLOGIC TIME SPAN: Jurassic Period, 152 to 150 million years ago

FOSSIL TYPE: Body fossil, trace fossil (footprints)

Titanoboa

SAY IT! *TIE-tan-OH-boa*

In 2009, paleontologists in La Guajira, Colombia, discovered what looked like the backbone of a snake, except it was *huge*. What they had found was the first fossil of *Titanoboa* (means "Titanic boa"), which was once the world's largest snake. *Titanoboa* was 12.8 meters (42 feet) long—twice as long as a giraffe is tall—and weighed 1,135 kilograms (2,500 pounds).

Paleontologists have since discovered fossils of at least 28 *Titanoboa* individuals in the Cerrejón coal mine in La Guajira, Colombia. More than 2,000 plant fossils discovered at the site revealed that *Titanoboa* lived in the tropical South American rain forest, which was much hotter than today's rain forests (86 to 93 degrees Fahrenheit/30 to 34 degrees Celsius).

FOSSIL STATS

ORDER: Squamata

FAMILY: Boidae

GENUS: *Titanoboa*

GEOLOGIC TIME SPAN: Paleocene Epoch, 60 to 58 million years ago

FOSSIL TYPE: Body fossil

Aepyornis maximus ("Elephant bird")

SAY IT! *AY-pee-OR-nis MAX-i-muss*

Aepyornis (means "high bird") was one of the largest birds to ever walk the Earth. That's right, walk! *Aepyornis* was a **ratite**, a flightless bird, that was related to ostriches, emus, rheas, and kiwis. *Aepyornis maximus* is nicknamed the "Elephant Bird" due to its size and strength; it weighed 210 to 340 kilograms (460 to 750 pounds) and stood 3 meters (10 feet) tall.

Aepyornis fossils, bones, and eggs have been discovered only on Madagascar, an island in the Indian Ocean. One egg from *Aepyornis* is 34 centimeters (13 inches) long—it could fit 120 to 150 chicken eggs inside it. (That's one big omelet!) Elephant birds went extinct around a thousand years ago. There are only about 40 complete elephant bird eggs in museums today.

FOSSIL STATS

ORDER: Aepyornithiformes

FAMILY: Aepyornithidae

GENUS: *Aepyornis*

GEOLOGIC TIME SPAN: Holocene Epoch, 1000 to 100 CE

FOSSIL TYPE: Body fossil

FOSSIL DISCOVERIES

Raphus cucullatus ("Dodo")

SAY IT! *RAPH-us CUCK-cull-LA-tus*

Raphus cucullatus (means "hooded bustard"), commonly known as the dodo bird, was a flightless bird that lived on the island of Mauritius in the Indian Ocean. Dodo birds were a giant relative of pigeons but were unlike anything alive today. Fully grown dodos were 1 meter (3 feet) tall and weighed 10.6 to 17.5 kilograms (23 to 39 pounds).

In 1598, European sailors landed on the island of Mauritius. Since dodo birds had no fear of humans, the hungry sailors easily hunted the birds for food. Other animals the sailors brought with them destroyed the dodos' nests and competed with them for food and shelter. By 1680, dodo birds were extinct. There are only a few complete dodo skeletons in museums today.

FOSSIL STATS

ORDER: Columbiformes

FAMILY: Columbidae

GENUS: *Raphus*

GEOLOGIC TIME SPAN: Pleistocene Epoch, 1 million years ago to 1693 CE

FOSSIL TYPE: Body fossil

Mammuthus primigenius ("Woolly mammoth")

SAY IT! *MAM-muh-thus pry-mih-JEN-ee-us*

Mammuthus primigenius (means "first mammoth") evolved 400,000 years ago in East Asia and lived during the Ice Age, or Pleistocene Epoch, and into the Holocene Epoch. This relative of today's Asian elephant stood between 2.7 and 3.4 meters (9 and 11 feet) tall and weighed 6 metric tons (6.6 tons). Woolly mammoths were covered in a coat of thick, brown fur that kept them warm in the Ice Age's freezing climate, and they ate grasses.

Woolly mammoths went extinct around 2000 BCE. Their frozen (not fossilized) carcasses have been discovered thawing out of the permafrost in Siberia and Alaska. One of the best places in the world to see mammoth skeletons is at the University of Nebraska State Museum in Lincoln, Nebraska.

FOSSIL STATS

ORDER: Proboscidea

FAMILY: Elephantidae

GENUS: *Mammuthus*

GEOLOGIC TIME SPAN: Pleistocene Epoch, 400,000 to 4,000 years ago

FOSSIL TYPE: Body fossil

Australopithecus afarensis ("Lucy")

SAY IT! *AUS-tra-LO-pith-uh-cuss a-far-EN-sis*

"Lucy" was the first fossil hominin (human relative) discovered that walked upright on two legs, like humans. She was small, standing 1.1 meters (3 feet, 7 inches) tall and weighing 29 kilograms (64 pounds), and this along with the fossil remains of her pelvis tell us she was probably a female. Her skeleton is 40 percent complete—great for a hominin!

Lucy was discovered on November 24, 1974, in Ethiopia by anthropologist Dr. Donald Johanson. She was named "Lucy" after the Beatles song, "Lucy in the Sky with Diamonds" (it was playing in camp the day she was found). Lucy's fossils are now housed at the National Museum of Ethiopia in Addis Ababa, Africa.

FOSSIL STATS

ORDER: Primates

FAMILY: Hominidae

GENUS: *Australopithecus*

GEOLOGIC TIME SPAN: Pliocene Epoch, 3.2 million years ago

FOSSIL TYPE: Body fossil, trace fossil (footprints)

FAMOUS FOSSIL HUNTERS

Mary Anning, who was born in 1799 in Lyme Regis in Dorset, England, was one of the world's first paleontologists. Mary and her family collected fossils along the cliffs and beach near their home, where Anning found ammonites, belemnites, and fossil bones. The family sold these fossil curiosities to tourists to earn money.

When Mary was 12 years old, she and her brother Joseph discovered a complete *Ichthyosaurus* skeleton. By age 24, Mary had found the world's first complete *Plesiosaurus*. Then, in 1828, she discovered the first pterosaur ever found in England—*Dimorphodon*.

Mary Anning's discoveries have helped establish the theory of extinction and the science of paleontology. Her passion and love for fossils made her one of the world's first (and best) paleontologists in history.

Glaucus atlanticus,
the blue dragon sea slug

Chapter Four

ALL ABOUT INVERTEBRATES

When you think of an animal, what do you picture in your mind? Is it a cat, a bird, a fish? Those animals all share something in common—they have backbones, which means they are vertebrates. But the animal kingdom includes so much more.

What is an Invertebrate?

Did you know that 97 percent of all animals on Earth are invertebrates?

Invertebrates are a group of animals that have soft bodies without bones. They don't have an internal skeleton like you do. Instead, some have an **exoskeleton**. This means that their skeleton is on the outside of their bodies rather than on the inside. An exoskeleton is a hard, protective covering made from minerals and proteins. Some exoskeletons use a protein called **chitin** [KY-tin], whereas others form a shell made from calcium carbonate [KAL-see-um CAR-bun-ate] or aragonite [ah-RAG-oh-nyte]. Insects and crabs have chitin exoskeletons, whereas clams or oysters have calcium carbonate and aragonite shells.

Where Invertebrates Come From

Invertebrates first evolved in the oceans of the Precambrian Period (500 million years ago). The first invertebrates were soft-bodied animals that initially lacked the protection of an outer covering, but they soon evolved to have hard, protective exoskeletons. By the Paleozoic Era (541 to 251 million years ago), the oceans teemed with different kinds of invertebrate life—many of which still exist today.

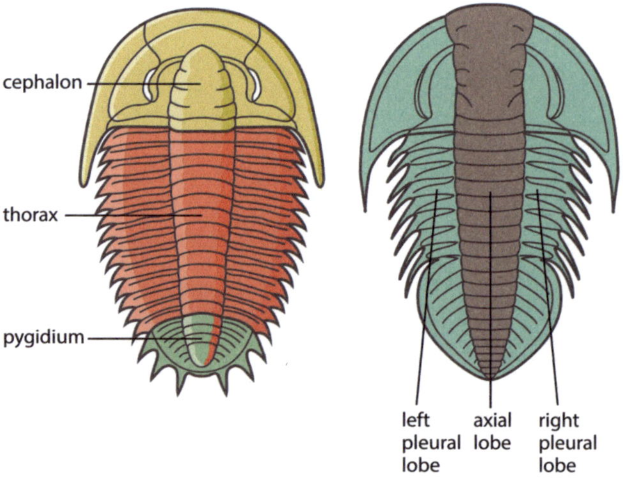

Many of the invertebrates in this chapter spend their lives buried in, or on top of, a seabed. After they die, the minerals from water and mud preserve their shells, which don't decay easily. (These shells can eventually become fossils.) The soft parts of an invertebrate animal, such as the tentacles of a squid or the gills of a trilobite, usually decompose, but sometimes they can be preserved in fine detail.

How Invertebrates Live

Many invertebrates, such as octopuses, live by themselves, whereas other invertebrates, like corals, live together in large groups called colonies. Corals live in a colony that they build together by sharing their exoskeletons—like a coral apartment complex. Living in groups is one reason why many kinds

of invertebrates are found as fossils together, especially corals.

Invertebrates lay eggs and can produce hundreds, thousands, or even millions of eggs. The modern bigfin reef squid (*Sepioteuthis lessoniana*) can lay 1,000 to 6,000 eggs at a time. Adult invertebrates produce millions of offspring. This is why there are so many more invertebrates than vertebrates.

Many invertebrates live in the water where sediment is deposited. As tiny particles of sediment rain down on the ocean floor, the animals that live there can become buried—unless they become another animal's dinner! These buried animals can become fossilized pretty easily, much more easily than animals that live on land.

Where to Find Invertebrate Fossils

Trilobites, brachiopods, gastropods, ammonites, and nautiloids are the most common groups of invertebrates that you can find as fossils. Why are they so common whereas other fossils are not?

Most of the invertebrate fossils you'll learn about are found in sedimentary rocks from the oceans of the Paleozoic Era (542 to 251 million years ago). Over time, waters once teeming with invertebrate life became buried under sediment as the Earth's rocks and land masses shifted, moved, and became exposed. This is a scientific theory called plate tectonics. As the Earth's tectonic plates continued to move, some oceans dried up while new ones formed. What was once an ocean floor might eventually move to the top of a mountain. This is why we find fossils that used to live in the ocean now on land, even on top of Mount Everest!

Erosion from water, wind, and glaciers eventually expose these Paleozoic oceans' rocks, revealing the fossils hidden within. These rocky outcrops are great places to look for invertebrate ocean fossils. Sometimes thousands can be found in a single area.

Over the past 600 million years, invertebrates have evolved into an amazing diversity of body forms—from squiggly worms to stinging wasps and everything in between There are more invertebrates than we can even count, so explore them on your own!

MEET THE MODERN INVERTEBRATES

ANNELIDS are segmented or ringed worms.

ARTHROPODS include crustaceans, insects, spiders, and scorpions.

BRACHIOPODS are also called lampshells.

BRYOZOA are known as moss animals.

CNIDARIANS include aquatic life like jellyfish and sea anemones.

ECHINODERMS are symmetrical marine animals like sea stars, sea cucumbers, and sea urchins.

MOLLUSKS are part of a large phylum that includes gastropods, cephalopods, and bivalves.

NEMATODA is a phylum of worm-like animals that include nematodes, or roundworms.

PLATYHELMINTHES include flatworms.

PORIFERA include sponges.

ROTIFERS include an aquatic group also known as "wheel animals."

Trilobites

SAY IT! *TRY-low-bites*

Trilobites (means "three lobes") are a group of invertebrates that first evolved in the Cambrian Period (521 million years ago) and were the dominant **arthropods** [ARE-throw-pods] in the oceans for more than 252 million years. There were once more than 15,000 different species of trilobites, and they ranged in size from a grain of sand to the size of a basketball.

These extinct arthropods lived in the ocean. They had two big eyes and a hard, protective exoskeleton that was divided into three main sections called lobes. Over millions of years, trilobites evolved different exoskeletons that could live in various environments. Some could roll up into a ball (like an armadillo) in order to protect themselves against predators. Trilobites went extinct at the end of the Permian Period (252 million years ago).

FOSSIL STATS

PHYLUM: Arthropoda

CLASS: Trilobita

SPECIES: *Asaphus kowalewskii*

GEOLOGIC TIME SPAN: Cambrian Period to Permian Period, 521 to 252 million years ago

FOSSIL TYPE: Body fossils, molds and casts, trackways

Brachiopods

SAY IT! *BRACK-ee-oh-pods*

Brachiopods (means "arm foot") are common fossils that resemble clams but are in a phylum (group of animals) called lampshells. Like clams, they have a shell with two parts and a hinge that encloses their body. But whereas clams are divided in half horizontally, brachiopods are split vertically along the top (dorsal) and bottom (ventral) halves. Most brachiopods attach themselves to something and then never move again (or, if they do, it's not very far). When a brachiopod dies, it becomes buried in the sediment in which it lived.

Brachiopods have been evolving since the early Cambrian Period (530 million years ago). Most, like *Unispirifer* [YOU-ni-SPEER-if-ir], are so small they can fit in your hand. There are 300 species of brachiopods still living today.

FOSSIL STATS

PHYLUM: Brachiopoda

CLASSES: Inarticulata and Articulata

GEOLOGIC TIME SPAN: Cambrian Period to now, 541 million years ago to present

FOSSIL TYPE: Body fossils, molds and casts, trackways

FOSSIL DISCOVERIES

FOSSIL DISCOVERIES

Gastropods

SAY IT! *GAS-tro-pods*

Gastropods (means "stomach foot") are the largest and most successful group of mollusks. What's a mollusk? Mollusks are soft-bodied animals; many have a calcium carbonate shell either inside or outside their body. Mollusks include both the snails in your garden and the brightly colored nudibranchs [NEW-dih-braynk] (sea slugs) in the ocean as well as many others.

The first gastropods appear in the fossil record around the late Cambrian Period and thrived in the Ordovician Period [OR-do-vish-ee-an] (485 to 443 million years ago). Gastropods live in both fresh and salt water, and their shells fossilize easily because they are made of the mineral calcium carbonate. There are 15,000 known fossil species and up to 150,000 living species.

FOSSIL STATS

PHYLUM: Mollusca

CLASS: Gastropoda

SPECIES: *Chromodoris elisabethina*

GEOLOGIC TIME SPAN: Cambrian Period to now, 500 million years ago to present

FOSSIL TYPE: Body fossils, molds and casts, trackways

Ammonites

SAY IT! *AM-on-ites*

Ammonites (means "horns of Ammon") are an extinct group of cephalopods, marine animals related to cuttlefish, squid, and octopuses. The name ammonite comes from the Egyptian god Ammon, who had the spiral horns of a ram. Ammonites evolved in the Devonian Period (405 million years ago) and went extinct 66 million years ago during the Cretaceous-Paleogene extinction.

Ammonites had septa, divisions inside the shell that made them stronger. Although most ammonites were small enough to hold in your hand, some were huge. The largest ammonite was *Parapuzosia* [Pah-rah-poo-ZOH-see-ah]. It was 2.2 meters (7 feet) wide—as long as a Volkswagen Beetle! All ammonites were predators; they ate other animals like plankton, fish, and crustaceans, but ammonites were also prey for fish, ichthyosaurs, and mosasaurs!

FOSSIL STATS

PHYLUM: Mollusca

CLASS: Cephalopoda

SPECIES: *Arnioceras semicostatum*

GEOLOGIC TIME SPAN: Devonian Period to Cretaceous Period, 409 to 66 million years ago

FOSSIL TYPE: Body fossils, molds and casts, trackways

Nautiloids

SAY IT! *NOT-til-oids*

Nautiloids are a type of marine cephalopod and are related to ammonites, cuttlefish, octopuses, and squids. Nautiloids first evolved in the late Cambrian Period and lived alongside ammonites. They had tentacles, two eyes, and though they started out with straight, pointed shells, over time their shells became more curled and coiled, much like the nautilus you see today.

Nautilus use jet-propulsion to swim. They draw water in and out of their shell, then expel the water through their hyponome (a tube inside their shell) to propel themselves. Nautilus can move at a speed of 2 knots (2 miles per hour).

Nautiloids survived many extinctions and are still with us. There are 2,500 species of nautiloids in the fossil record. Six species, such as the chambered nautilus, still live in the oceans today.

FOSSIL STATS

PHYLUM: Mollusca

CLASS: Cephalopoda

SPECIES: *Nautilus pompilius*

GEOLOGIC TIME SPAN: Cambrian Period to now, 500 million years ago to present

FOSSIL TYPE: Body fossils, molds and casts, trackways

EXCITING FINDS: EDIACARAN FOSSILS

In 1946, Australian geologist Reginald Sprigg was exploring the Ediacara Hills in South Australia when he found what looked like impressions of fossilized jellyfish in sandstone dating back to 560 to 541 million years ago. No one had ever found fossils that old before, especially with soft-tissue impressions! But when he wrote a paper about his discovery, the scientific community rejected it. They didn't believe him.

We now know this fossil as *Dickinsonia*. It was only after the discovery of *Charnia* [CHAR-nee-ah] (another soft-bodied fossil) in England in 1956 that Reginald's discoveries were finally taken seriously.

Reginald's Ediacaran fossils are now considered the best example of soft-bodied fossils in the world. In fact, this time period was named the Ediacaran Period (after the Ediacara Hills), and the *Spriggina* [Sprihg-GEEN-ah] fossil from these hills was named for Reginald Sprigg.

Ginkgo biloba fossils

Chapter Five

ALL ABOUT PLANTS

Let's turn over a new leaf and talk about plants. What would humans do without plants? The grass you wiggle your toes in, the air you breathe, and even the food you eat are all possible because of plants. Can you think of all the different ways you use plants?

How Plants Make Food

Plants make their own food through a process called photosynthesis [FOE-toe-SIN-the-SIS]. This means that their leaves and roots absorb sunlight, carbon dioxide gas, and water and turn it all into a type of sugar called glucose. This process is called the Calvin Cycle. Plants release oxygen (one of the gasses we need to breathe) as a result of this cycle. The Great Oxygenation Event (3 to 1 billion years ago) is what gave the Earth its oxygen-rich atmosphere.

Algae

The first plant-like organism was algae [AL-gee], which evolved in the Precambrian Period (at least 1.2 billion years ago). Algae was the first food source for many Cambrian animals and helped the first invertebrates flourish and diversify during the Cambrian explosion.

Mosses and Liverworts

In the Paleozoic Era (541 to 252 million years ago), plants moved from water to the land where they greatly diversified. By the Ordovician Period (470 million years ago), mosses, hornworts, and liverworts were the first to evolve branching roots called rhizoids, which held them fast to the ground, much like plant roots today.

Gymnosperms

In the warm, tropical climate of the Carboniferous Period (358 million years ago), there grew thick forests of giant horsetails, club mosses, and fern and scale trees with towering canopies like Lepidodendron. By the Permian Period (299 million years ago), the gymnosperms—plants that include conifers, cycads, and *Ginkgo*—had evolved to produce cones that protected their seeds.

Angiosperms

By the early Cretaceous Period (140 million years ago), the first angiosperms [AN-jee-OH-spurms] had evolved, and they appear in the fossil record. These flowering plants contained the first small flowers and fruit. Animals fed on the pollen and fruit, which spread these plants across the land. For example, bees spread pollen from flower to flower and herbivores (plant eaters) such as dinosaurs, birds, and other mammals ate the fruit. As the seeds passed through the animals' digestive systems, the nutrient-rich scat (poop) dropped to the ground and the seeds within took root, spreading the plants.

Why Are Plant Fossils Rare?

Any part of a plant can become a fossil—roots, trunks, stems, leaves, branches, sap, flowers, fruits, and even pollen. These fossils can be as tiny as a grain of pollen or as big as a tree! But plants usually live on the forest floor, which isn't a great place for fossilization to occur. Insects, worms, and fungi can either eat the fallen leaves or the leaves will decompose and turn into soil. This doesn't leave much of the plant to fossilize.

The best plant fossils form in ancient lakebeds where the low oxygen levels prevented leaves, bark, cones, and other plant materials from decomposing. Florissant Fossil Beds National Park, an ancient fossilized lakebed in Colorado, is one of the best places to see fossilized plants.

PALEOBOTANY

The study of plant fossils is called paleobotany [PAY-lee-oh-BOT-an-ee]. When we study plants, we learn amazing things about ancient environments—what the temperature was like, how much rain fell, and what lived during that period in time. For example, fossil plants tell us that ice-covered Antarctica was a rain forest only 23 million years ago!

What can you learn from the plants around you today?

Stromatolites

SAY IT! *STROH-mat-oh-lites*

Fossil stromatolites (means "layered rock") are lumps of sedimentary rocks that formed between layers of microscopic cyanobacteria ("blue-green algae") and bits of calcium carbonate or limestone from ocean sediment. Stromatolites began forming in the Archean Eon (3.5 billion years ago).

Why is the fossil record full of fossil stromatolites? One hypothesis is that there weren't animals around to feed on them yet.

Stromatolites continue to form in the extremely salt-rich lagoons in Brazil, Mexico, the Bahamas, and in Shark Bay in Western Australia. The stromatolites in these lagoons look just like they did billions of years ago.

THE GREAT OXYGENATION EVENT

The air we breathe today is made of oxygen and other gasses, but the Earth didn't always have enough oxygen for us to survive. How did this happen? The answer is: cyanobacteria [sigh-ANN-oh-back-TEER-ee-ah].

Cyanobacteria are microscopic bacteria that produce their own food through photosynthesis; in the process, they release "waste" in the form of oxygen. During the Proterozoic Eon (2.4 to 2.1 billion years ago), cyanobacteria across the world released so much oxygen that iron particles in the oceans began to oxidize (rust), forming an iron oxide. This period is known as the Great Oxygenation Event. It increased oxygen in the air, which changed the Earth's plants, soil, and water in a way that allowed new organisms to surface and thrive.

Evidence of this event can be seen in what is called banded iron rock formations. This streaky, colorful sedimentary rock dates from the Precambrian Period; look closely and you'll see red bands (that's the iron oxide) in between gray layers (sediment). The largest banded iron formations are in western Minnesota, Australia, Greenland, and Brazil.

Lepidodendron

SAY IT! *LEP-id-oh-DEN-dron*

Lepidodendron (means "scale tree") was an extinct relative of the club mosses that evolved during the Carboniferous Period (315 to 300 million years ago). *Lepidodendron* was quite large—it reached 2 meters (7 feet) to 30 meters (98 feet) in height and more than 1 meter (3 feet) in diameter.

Lepidodendron was not a true moss; it was a vascular plant called a lycophyte that looked different from its living relatives, the club mosses, firmmosses, and quillworts. The trunks were probably green and full of chlorophyll, more like leaves, and they reproduced through spores, like ferns. *Lepidodendron* is known as the "scale tree" due to the diamond-shaped scars left by the leaves that grew from the trunk.

FOSSIL STATS

ORDER: Lepidodendrales

FAMILY: Lepidodendraceae

GENUS: *Lepidodendron*

GEOLOGIC TIME SPAN: Early Carboniferous Period to late Triassic Period, 359 to 205 million years ago

FOSSIL TYPE: Bark, branches, leaves, trunks, roots, spores

Ginkgo biloba

SAY IT! *GINK-oh-by-LOW-buh*

Did you know that a tree once eaten by dinosaurs still grows in your neighborhood? The *Ginkgo biloba* (means "silver apricot") is a common tree that is called a "living fossil" because it's been growing on Earth for almost 200 million years. These trees can grow to be 20 to 35 meters (66 to 115 feet) tall and their fossilized leaves have been found in geologic formations that span many geologic time periods across the world.

The only species of *Ginkgo* alive today is *Ginkgo biloba*. *Ginkgo biloba* are popular in neighborhoods and cities because they have beautiful leaves. They also produce fruit and nuts used in traditional Chinese cooking and medicine. You may not have to travel far to see one of these ancient trees; just look around your neighborhood.

FOSSIL STATS

ORDER: Ginkgoales

FAMILY: Ginkgoaceae

GENUS: *Ginkgo*

GEOLOGIC TIME SPAN: Jurassic Period to now, 190 million years ago to present

FOSSIL TYPE: Bark, branches, leaves, trunks, fruits

Alethopteris sp.

SAY IT! *AL-eth-op-tur-is*

Alethopteris is an extinct plant that was related to cycads [SIGH-kads]. *Alethopteris* fossils date back to the Carboniferous Period (360 million years ago) to the early Cretaceous Period (113 million years ago). This tree-like plant had fronds (leaves) that could grow up to 7 meters (23 feet) long; the whole plant could grow to be 10 meters (33 feet) tall. *Alethopteris* fossil leaves are found in different geologic formations worldwide.

Alethopteris and other Carboniferous Period plants evolved a substance called lignin [LIHG-nihn], and this made their stems strong and resistant to decay. Over time, and under lots of heat and pressure, these dead plants turned in to coal. The "lead" in a pencil comes from a form of coal called graphite. This means that you can write your homework with a fossil plant.

FOSSIL STATS

ORDER: Medullosales

FAMILY: Alethopteridae

GENUS: *Alethopteris*

GEOLOGIC TIME SPAN: Carboniferous Period to early Cretaceous Period, 360 to 113 million years ago

FOSSIL TYPE: Bark, branches, leaves, trunks, roots

FOSSIL DISCOVERIES

FOSSIL DISCOVERIES

Araucaria mirabilis

SAY IT! *AH-raw-care-eeya meer-a-bill-iss*

Conifers, or pine trees, are very common; we even use them to celebrate holidays, such as Christmas. *Araucaria* are a group of conifers that evolved in the Jurassic Period. These pine trees range from 5 to 80 meters (16 to 262 feet) tall and were a favorite food of long-necked sauropod dinosaurs, including *Diplodocus*. Pine trees are gymnosperms [JIM-no-SPIRMS], or plants that produce seeds without a hard outer cover. Conifers have needle-shaped leaves and pine cones, which hold and then release the seeds in order to reproduce.

There are more than 600 species of conifers alive today. Most of the petrified trees at Petrified Forest National Park in Arizona are from extinct relatives of *Araucaria*, but living *Araucaria* are found in the forests of New Caledonia, eastern Australia, and South America.

FOSSIL STATS

ORDER: Pinales

FAMILY: Araucariaceae

GENUS: *Araucaria*

GEOLOGIC TIME SPAN: Jurassic Period to now, 168 million years ago to present

FOSSIL TYPE: Bark, branches, leaves, trunks, roots, cone

Sassafras

SAY IT! *SASS-ah-FRASS*

When you bite into a piece of fruit, you are eating the fruit of an angiosperm. Angiosperms, or flowering plants, are the most diverse group of plants alive today with more than 300,000 known species. All fruits and many vegetables are produced by angiosperms.

The first angiosperms evolved in the early Cretaceous Period (140 million years ago). *Sassafras* are large trees that grow 9 to 35 meters (30 to 115 feet) tall—as high as a 10-story building! *Sassafras* trees have three different leaf shapes—one leaf shape even looks like the footprint of a three-toed theropod dinosaur.

Sassafras trees produce fruit eaten by birds and mammals, but people also use the bark and roots to make a delicious drink—root beer! Today *Sassafras albidum* grows in the eastern forests of the United States and Asia.

FOSSIL STATS

ORDER: Laurales

FAMILY: Lauraceae

GENUS: *Sassafras*

GEOLOGIC TIME SPAN: Late Cretaceous Period to now, 105 million years ago to present

FOSSIL TYPE: Bark, branches, leaves, trunks, roots

MAKE YOUR OWN PLANT FOSSIL

The materials you need:

- small leaf
- 12-by-12-inch square of parchment paper
- flat surface
- air-dry clay (available from a local craft store)
- small bowl of water
- toothpick

How to make the fossil:

1. Go outside and collect any small leaf, then bring it home.
2. Once inside, grab the parchment paper and lay it on a flat surface.
3. Roll the clay into a few small balls and press them flat onto the paper.
4. Dip your finger in the water and sprinkle a few drops onto the clay.
5. Now take your leaf and press it lightly onto the surface of the clay.
6. Use a toothpick to carefully remove the leaf from the clay.
7. Put the clay somewhere safe and let it air-dry for 24 to 48 hours.

Your piece of clay will hold an impression of the leaf. Now, use your homemade "fossil" to find out which plant species your leaf came from!

MORE TO DISCOVER

RECOMMENDED WEBSITES

Montana Dinosaur Trail
MTDinoTrail.org

National Geologic Map Database
Ngmdb.usgs.gov

Paleontology, American Museum of Natural History
AMNH.org/explore/ology/paleontology

Understanding Evolution, University of California Museum of Paleontology
Evolution.berkeley.edu

RECOMMENDED BOOKS

Asteroid Impact, by Douglas Henderson

Cruisin' the Fossil Freeway: An Epoch Tale of a Scientist and an Artist on the Ultimate 5,000-Mile Paleo Road Trip, by Kirk Johnson and Ray Troll

Dinosaur Art: The World's Greatest Paleoart, by Steve White

Dinosaurs: The Most Complete, Up-to-Date Encyclopedia for Dinosaur Lovers of All Ages, by Dr. Thomas R. Holtz Jr.

National Audubon Society Field Guide to North American Fossils, by National Audubon Society Field Guides

The World of Dinosaurs: An Illustrated Tour, by Mark A. Norell

GLOSSARY

AGNATHANS (AG-nath-ans): Jawless vertebrates with a skeleton and notochord made of cartilage.

ARTHROPODS (AR-throw-pods): Invertebrates that have jointed legs and a hard exoskeleton made of chitin.

AVIAN (EY-vee-uhn): Bird or birdlike

CHITIN (KY-tin): A protein that forms the exoskeleton of an invertebrate animal.

CLADE (Klayde): A group of animals that shares a common ancestor.

EROSION (ih-ROH-zhuhn): When water, wind, ice, or gravity breaks down and moves sediment (soil, rocks, sand) from one place to another.

EXOSKELETON (ek-sow-SKEH-luh-tn): The hard outer cuticle or shell of an invertebrate that provides protection and support.

EXTINCT: An organism that does not have any living individuals left.

FOSSIL RECORD: The history of life on Earth as documented by fossils.

FURCULA (FUR-cue-luh): The "wishbone" found in birds and other dinosaurs; the clavicle or collarbone in humans.

GEOLOGIC TIME: The age of the Earth and sections of it determined by studying layers of rock through radiometric dating.

ICHTHYOSAURS (ICK-thee-oh-sores): Extinct marine reptiles distantly related to dinosaurs that looked similar to a dolphin.

MOSASAURS (MOSE-a-sores): Extinct marine reptiles distantly related to dinosaurs that are related to modern snakes and monitor lizards.

NOTOCHORD (NOTE-oh-kord): A flexible spine-like structure made of cartilage found in some groups of vertebrates; helps give structure to the body.

ORGANISM (ORGAN-ism): Any living thing; animals, plants, fungi, and single-celled organisms.

PALEONTOLOGY (PAY-lee-an-tall-a-gee): The study of life on Earth through fossils.

PERMAFROST (PERM-ah-frawst): A thick layer of soil that stays frozen year-round; found in the Arctic and Antarctic.

PERMINERALIZATION (PURR-mineral-eye-say-shun): A process of fossilization where water carries dissolved minerals into spaces where they crystalize and fill the place of living tissue.

PLACODERMS (PLACK-oh-DERMS): Fish with solid plates of bones covering their heads.

RADIOMETRIC DATING: Studying the steady rate of decay of radioactive elements within the sediment to determine the age of the layers of the Earth.

RATITE (RAT-ahyt): A group of flightless birds (ostrich, emu, rhea, cassowary, kiwi, moa, and elephant bird).

SEDIMENTARY (sed-uh-MEN-tuh-ree): A type of rock formed in layers through erosion by water or air.

TETRAPODS (TEH-truh-pods): Vertebrate animals with four limbs. Snakes are an exception, as they lost their arms and legs through time.

INDEX

ABOUT THE AUTHOR

ASHLEY HALL is a paleontologist, naturalist, and science educator and communicator who is passionate about teaching everyone about the natural world. She received a Bachelor of Arts in Anthropology and Animal Behavior from Indiana University Bloomington. She has spent the majority of her career educating the public about natural history and paleontology through tours and programs at the Los Angeles Zoo, Natural History Museum of Los Angeles County, and the La Brea Tar Pits. As Assistant Curator of Paleontology at the Raymond M. Alf Museum of Paleontology, she excavated, identified, and helped care for the museum's fossil collection. Ashley enjoys sharing her knowledge of natural history through her social media platforms. She is a talented speaker and gives workshops on how to communicate science through social media. She is dedicated to making sure paleontology is accessible for all. She and her husband, Lee, love spending time exploring museums and nature together.